Before They Were Songs

A Musician's Love Poems To His Muse

Before They Were Songs

A Musician's Love Poems To His Muse

Douglas Wayne Jessop

Harlow's Publishing House
2014

Copyright © 2014 by Douglas Wayne Jessop

All rights reserved. This book or any portion thereof may not be reproduced or used in any manner whatsoever without the express written permission of the publisher except for the use of brief quotations in a book review or scholarly journal.

First Printing: 2014

ISBN: 978-0-9906989-0-6

Harlow's Publishing House
1910 Hillcrest Road

Los Angeles, California 90068

www.douglasjessopmusic.com

Dedication

To Johanna Martina Ulrika:

Friend, Lover, Muse and Wife.

Contents

Acknowledgements ix

Introduction xi

Know That My Heart 1

On The Road 2

When I Think 4

A Night Without You 5

Your Light Comes To Me 7

All Is Going As Planned 8

Without You 9

Yes…. 11

We Are Running Now 12

Feeling You 13

We Sleep 14

The Cat Is Back 15

If You Are Lucky 16

There Are Angels Among Us 18

We Formally Agreed	19
A Muse	20
All Loves	21
Waiting To See You	22
I Thought	23
Sometimes	25
Heart Still Beating	27
In The Quiet Moments	28
The Hunter Cat	29
We Stole Moments	30
A Day Without Poetry	32
The Moment is Perfect	34
Poetry Will Soon Resume	35
As You Held Me	36
Journey of Love	39
No One Tells You	41
Does The Universe Test Us	42
If There Is A Quiet Time	44
I Have Poured My Heart	45
Alone	46
Dearest Fleur	47

The Poetry	49
We All Want Magic In Our Lives	50
My True Heart Is Now In Charge	52
My Heart	53
If I Take The Time	54
Day Is Flying By	55
Alone Today	56
Not A Day Goes By	57
Cat Hiding In A Cupboard	58
Sitting Here Guitar In Hand	59
What Is Love Now	60
You Are Sleeping	61
Maybe This Rush	62
I Miss You	64
Alone Tonight	65
An Old Business Aquaintance	68
Missing You	69
My Cat Says	70
How Many Ways	71
Home Late	72
Lovers Approach	73

Some Days 75

One's Ability To Love..76

My Lips 77

Just A Sheet Of Paper 78

Small Smooth Thoughts 80

Thought I Might Be...81

There Isn't Much Time 82

You Ask Me 83

Thinking About Dreams 87

To Wake Up To You 90

Acknowledgements

I would like to thank Noreen Nash for her encouragement and shining example of all that is beautiful, good and right in the world.

Introduction

There is a lot of water under my bridge – I've been an actor, dancer, short order cook, janitor, lawyer, professor, father and divorcé (after 29 years). In a dramatic "do-over" of life, I closed my Colorado law office in 2009 (after 25 years of practice) and moved to Los Angeles to study music.

Moving to Hollywood meant following the "whim"- which in this case meant guitar – an instrument I have played over 50 years. This in turn led me to writing and singing my own songs.

Ulrika was my first Los Angeles friend in Hollywood. After about three years of close proximity, we ventured to deepen our connection. These poems were written during the following two years of my life with the-neighbor-who-became-my-wife.

I have always written words but I did not know that my writings were "poems." It was just how I have always written, especially when trying to express where I was at the moment. It was important for me to just sit and take the time to listen.

At the urging of my muse and friends, this little book was born. I cannot say why this book must travel but travel it must. Written alone, it will take its journey to you alone.

Know That My Heart

Know that my heart trembles
As I approach
This improbable meeting
That fate long decided
Two souls
Stretching to really see
A new truth
Past layers of life
Past the sins of omission and
commission
The generous and selfish moments
The selves given away foolishly
To those who would not see us
The wounds and beautiful scars
Past the real joys and moments of
Intense happiness
We have gratefully tasted

If I look into your eyes
And they let me in
I will go softly
I will not be lost
Not now
Not this time

On The Road

On the road
I dream of home
Of trees and flowers
Hot coffee favorite mug
Skin warmed by morning sun
Waiting for you
To pass my step
On the way to your little shop
So I can say hello
And tell you how beautiful
You are today
Without you knowing
Without me knowing
How much I love you

It was a ritual
That I obeyed
All was right in the world
If I saw you go by
Each day a different dress
Each day like a different movie
Each day to see your brave smile
I marveled at your strength
To return to the little shop
Of dreams
Where only the special few
Will visit and take away a treasure
To turn into commodity
An essence of your delight
You probably need a shop girl
Who does not care
Whether beauty departs

Each night I asked myself
Are you home
How long
And looked for clues
Of your presence
Touching the hood of
Your car gently
to measure the engine heat
to guess how long were you home
Counting the evening lights
Looking to see if your cat
Is waiting for you
Listening to see if our neighbor
Is laughing merrily with you
to the happy voices
Of your guests
to your classical music
to your passionate Italian
or French or German
As you paced with your phone
Or sat on your porch

So I hid in plain sight
From myself
From you
And now I see
Only today
Your arms and kisses

When I Think

When I think
It cannot be more
It is
When I think
I cannot go on
I can
When I think of you
I am
More

A Night Without You

A night without you
And I am adrift
The world I knew
Solid routine
Gone
The new world with you
So tender I weep
At its delicate texture
So unknown I am startled
By each new minute
Magic and light
So physical
My lips cannot remember
Not touching yours
My body cannot remember
A life without you
My arms have no meaning
Without you in them
My heart's steady beat
Waiting for the pressure
Of your breasts against me
So we may beat in time
My breath
Awaiting your perfume.
In my island bed
alone
I dream of nothing else
While riding the waves
Of the new sea
Tossing me carelessly
Effortlessly
With unknowable power
Shaken to my core
My soul unleashed

The light so bright
I blink to shed the tears
Of my awakening

Your Light Comes To Me

Your light comes to me
And I am in a state of grace
Your eyes sing
Beautiful songs
With words
That only my soul knows
Like a foreigner
Who has come finally home
And hears the long forgotten
Tongue of his motherland
And shudders at the shock
Of recognition
Shakes at the impossibility
That it was all there
Has always been there
Waiting
Waiting
Waiting
Like tears

All Is Going As Planned

All is going as planned
So the universe confirms
Its own reality
Of beautiful accidents
Spooky coincidences
Surprise alignments
Happy coupling

Without You

Without you
The day is just day
Minutes are just minutes
Life is just life

Without you
It is sunny and warm
But I can not
Feel it

My hands want to play
But only with you
My guitar wants to sing
But only of you

Without you
I wait to breath
Until you are here
Safely in my arns

Without you
Your last kisses
Burn my lips
And I cannot taste

Your last kisses
Still claiming my skin
The notes ringing
Bells of holiday

Without you
The air's
Sweet caresses
Go unanswered

Without you now
There is nothing
But you
But you
But you

Yes

Yes
Two different worlds
Two different lives
Two different pasts
Two different paths
That crossed
Then joined

Truth
Face to face
Side by side
Spooning
Walking
Eyes ahead
Holding hands

Dream
One new world
One new life
One new future

One new path
Separate
Together
Happy

We Are Running Now

We are running now
Faster than ever before
Clouds streaming by
Our breaths
Catching
Over and over
We move
With no fatigue
Tiredness banished
Miles ago
Our lungs labor
Our rhythms together
Beating like hearts
In love
The mountain
We have chosen
So high
The summit
A distant dream
Endless ledges
Wait our arrival
Staggering views
And vertigo
For a second

Before running faster
Higher
Side by side
In love

Feeling You

Feeling you
Now
My breath
A slow motion gasp
My heart
Desperately beating
Alive
Suspended
Charging madly
Fingertips brushing
Impossibile
Smoothness
Skin to skin
Whispering
Shouting
Crying
Sighing
A lifetime
Of hunger
Gone
Kisses falling
Like rose
Pedals
At midnight

Your scent
The warmth
Of coming
Home

We Sleep

We sleep
Like lovers
Dreaming
Waking to the slightest touch
Yielding to the rolling movement
Our bodies make
For us
Echoing the moments
The hours before
And predicting
Our future
Calling us
Pushing us
To the deep well
Within our souls
Where primal music
Is sung with muffled cries
Skin alive
We sleep
Like lovers

The Cat Is Back

The Cat is back in my bed
Like a king upon your pillow
Caressed by the soft breeze
Coming through the shaded window
Like the waving palm fronds
Of imaginary slaves
He looks up
As I come softly by
Both of us mildly startled
A bit pleased
By the other's presence
He receives my attention
To his ears with
Zen like acceptance
mixed with an undeniable
Small but measurable
Undercurrent
Of pleasure

Your scent still lingers in the air
And I am happily
taking care of business
Wrapping up the old life
Preparing for a new one

Waiting for you to come
Home

If You Are Lucky

If you are lucky
She comes to you
Like waves
Rising falling
Power beyond mortals
If you are lucky
She smiles
At the thought of you
And her face
Holds kindness for you
Like a perfect blanket
Wrapping you in warmth
If you are lucky
She holds your hand
With a presence
That stops all thought
That you are too late
For the love of your life
If you are lucky
She takes your urgent touch
With open arms
With jagged breath
Caught in open pleasure
With sloe eyes
That say everything
That receive everything
That hope for everything
If you are lucky
She calls your spirit
To rise with all the power
You are capable of
And you do
And crush yourself
Into the heat

That goes on and on
That goes on and on
If you are lucky

There Are Angels Among Us

There are angels among us
And if you are lucky
One may grow close to you
Do not question this gift
From heaven
Do not ask why
You were chosen
Do not think
Do not pretend

Enjoy
Life

With wings

We Formally Agreed

We formally agreed
In a moment
Of light and grace
To not touch
The beloved's
dearest parts
For a brief time
In our lifetime
Together
Now we suffer
The joy of angels

Heady with sensation
Speechless
The body soul
Has its day
Of triumph
When love
Is more
Than all history
Than all past
Attempts
To make meaning
Between two lovers
Two hearts
Two souls

A Muse

A muse
An angel in disguise
Graces me
With light
Only my soul
Can behold

Just knowing she is there
Puts music in my heart
Ancient rhythms
Soulful in the dark
Singing the melodies
Of living

Giants call me
To touch
The instruments
I am given
To play to the gods
In heaven

I pray my humble gifts
Are received

All Loves

All loves
Are secret
A color
Defined
By souls
Combined
Only they
Can see

No one
Can know
Their joy
Because
Simply
They are not
The same
Two lovers

It is hopeless
To explain
Yet
Yet
To you
I will not tire

Of holding
Our
Secret love

Waiting To See You

Waiting to see you
And hold you
The world's hue and cry
A distant memory
A faded roar
Just to imagine you
Consumes
Every fiber
Every cell
Every space
In me
I cry out
Wordlessly
Without sound
Breath caught
Deep within
The Muse
Plays my heart
Effortlessly
Passionately
The soul transfixed
At heaven's gate

I Thought

I thought
I was not looking
For true love
I was not looking
To be swept away
By emotions
Passion's burning fury
I was not looking
For any deeper meaning
Of life and soul

I thought
I had a simple life
A life of ease
Aloneness
Gently withstood
I thought
This was the way
Of the heart

But the heart
Did not tell me
That it knew
So much more

Laughing to itself
The stupidity of
"I thought"
While gently
Guiding me
Quietly
To you
Teaching me

To let go
Of selves
No longer needed

Letting me think
Whatever I wanted
Just as long
As I moved closer
To your eyes
Your lips

Your heart

And you
My beautiful neighbor
Visiting goddess
Out of reach

From another world
Enchanting
Vexing
Teasing
Your generous
Loving heart
Waiting

Sometimes

Sometimes
I speak too much
When the space
Between us
Is already full
Of love and passion
When your eyes
Are filled with
Mute acceptance
Gently reaching
For mine

Sometimes
I speak too much
When my eyes
Are filled with
Pictures of
Joyful love
My nerves
Flooded from
Gentle caresses

Sometimes
I speak too much
Because my brain
Does not trust
That you
Are really you
And that you
Could really feel
This way
About me

Sometimes

I speak too much
To hide
That I am
So new
To this kind
Of love

Heart Still Beating

Heart still beating
In the ears
That heard
The yes
In the chest
That felt
The yes
In the hands
That felt
The warmth
In the eyes
That saw the tears
Of yes
Yes
To my heart's
Soft calling
Will you be
My Love
My Muse
My Wife?

The echos
Of sweet yes
Still floating
Like a fine rain
Of flowers
Sun and clouds
Above
Miracles
Now possible

In The Quiet Moments

In the quiet moments
When clouds undress the moon
And motorized beasts
Lay quiet in their lairs
When the woody clack
Of bamboo
Plays the night wind song
And raccoons shuffle
Their pilgrimage
When appliances hum
Small themes of care
And palm fronds wave
Delicate fingers
Against the walls
I feel your heat
Next to mine
And for a moment

Life kisses me
Her son
As I kiss
Her sleeping gift

The Hunter Cat

The hunter cat
Fails to return
From his early morning rounds
Clouds dissolve the sun
Corners are examined
Hiding spots are searched
Neighborly kindness extended
The emptiness
Swallows our calls

We hold each other
Tenderly
There are no answers
No clever words
No insights
No future
Not today
Not from the heart
Of now

We Stole Moments

We stole moments
All day
Insisting on touching
Touching
Touching
Our bodies begging
Our thirst
Never ending

In the afternoon
We tear ourselves
From our sweetened bed
Called to the sea
To the beautiful sea

Primal Ocean
Stretching before us
The mist
Of crashing waves
Anoints our faces
With salted dew
 Suspended
Quietly happy
The tastes
Of pleasure
Still within us

Sun and skin
Embrace
Spirits soothed
Happily humming
The ocean's tireless
Caress of shore
Reminds

Now invites
Our throbbing rhythm
To its own

Our eyes
Meet
Wordlessly
Repeatedly
Our souls
Cannot
Stop
Smiling

A Day Without Poetry

A day without poetry
To you
Is like missing
The truth
A quiet meditation
On your being
The brilliant moment
Of grace
The shimmering white
Enveloping my soul
As I give thanks
For the joy and love
For the harmony
We share

Yes
I do not forget
Any of these things
When I am with you
It's just that
Stopping time
Is required
To let the passionate minutes
That have passed

Like a swollen river
Widening my shores
Flooding my plains
Time
To catch up
Inside
So I can
Face the swift current
Of delight

With you
Again
And again

The Moment Is Perfect

The moment is perfect
Even when we're not

As lovers are protected
From seeing at the start
The truth of each life
Grasped in a blink
The captured soul polaroid
Got it right we think
Until the past life collides
With the present
And our little horns
Signal our descent

The moment is perfect
Even when I'm not.

Poetry Will Soon Resume

Poetry will soon resume
The system is
Currently experiencing
Technical difficulties
Expression has been replaced
With life's demands
That apartments be moved
Accounts be changed
Broken are fixed
Dirt cleaned
Parents entertained
Dresses moved
Bicycles hung up
To remind us
To use them
At our leisure
After poetry
After moving furniture

As You Held Me

As you held me
The Dark Guardian
Tipped his hand
Perhaps
By accident
But I saw him
Blocking a door
I did not know
Was there
Did not know
Could open
And he saw me
What are you doing
Here
I cried
And then I knew
Old and hard
He had protected
Me
Faithfully all the years
Hiding me
So I could tell all
In truth
That my heart

Was open
Without suffering
The pain
Of love begun
So wrong
Of love gone
So wrong
Of love dead
In my arms

And now there is you
The lover muse
Whose passion demands
Surrender
Demands openness
Demands that
I come forward
To meet her
Fully
And until
Just now
I thought
I thought
I was a warrior
A lover
Fully there

The Dark Guardian
Fights me
Muffled bluntly
His blanketed resolve
Immovable at first
His advantage
Of stealth
Gone
His cloak slipping past
His eyes
And to his face
I plead my desire
To enter
The hidden portal
In search of
The deeper levels
Of heart and soul
With my love

And he listens
Testing my resolve
My strength
And waits a bit
For clarity
For deserved retirement

For a sense of rest
That comes from
Final accomplishment
The guarded
Now free

I stand in the opening
My breath caught
In small fists of air
Turning to you
To see me
And I am
In white
My long sleeves
Streaming
Hair blowing
Facing the sun
Of your love
Warming me
Through
And through
I turn again
To cross
The Darkness
To hopeful Light

Journey of Love

Journey of love
Blink of recognition
Ignites
The entire path
Seen
Understood
Desired
And like a dream
Left with the smoke
Of true fire

And slowly
I trace again
The outline of your face
The curve of your back
Drawing you over
And over
Feeling the power
Of the fingertips
To recognize
Truth and beauty
Each day
A simple day
Of meeting anew

A lover glimpsed
A friend foretold

Perhaps it is
A story
That writes
Itself
Each day
I wait

To discover
You
Me

Your sleepy warmth
Each morning
Each night
The touch of hands
The teasing smile
The dancing eyes
The dawning love
Growing
Finer
Delicate
Stronger

No One Tells You

No one tells you
How the heart
Will change
After months
In your lover's arms
How the simple
Currents of her awakening
Will run through you
Like your own
How her dreams
Will make sense
Like water flowing
Over smooth rocks
And tufted grass
Above the tree line
How her kisses
Will tell you
Everything
You are brave enough
To see and feel
How you will begin
To wordlessly understand
The ripples of color and light
That move across her face
How you will feel the heat
Of a hand that knows its heart
And scars you did not remember
Will emerge and heal
No one tells you

Does The Universe Test Us

Does the universe test us
When she delivers a blow
And drops us on the road
To hit the ground perfectly
And shatter like a mirror
Too late to tell
The future

Do I pass the test
If I close my eyes
And clench my teeth
To the cacophony
Of a shattered bone
Whining like a baby
And slowly exhale the air
That my lover and I
Had formerly shared
With such exuberance
But is now a burden
In my lungs
And turn and smile

Do you pass the test
If you keep coming home
To the lover in pain
And telling him your day
And including him in your
Stories
Deftly answering
The concerns of friends
Soothing him
With your softly radiant presence

No, the universe cares not
Maybe, I am
Yes, you are

If There Is A Quiet Time

If there is a quiet time
It comes softly
And sits with me
Listening to my breathing
The hum surrounds me
And all the sounds
Lose their grip
And I remember
The look in your eyes
When I hold you close
And I am falling
With all my heart
Through the stillness
And the languid air
Hushed
Your touch
Everywhere
And I have gone
Quietly
Again

I Have Poured My Heart

I have poured my heart
Into strings and wood
And for my effort
A voice was given
To teach me
To hear again

Heart soul
They speak as one
But I cannot hear
Tight chest
Pain crying out
Let me live again

My do over
Was so new
An adventure
With a small misstep
The road that had delighted
Became the muddy field
The blue skies obscured
The glasses thick
And dirty
Smudged and life

A poor blur
I hold the edges weakly
Struggling to feel
The simple joys
Of just being

Alone

Alone
Like before
Only different
I will see you again
After the daily doings
After the mindless rambles
After the conversations
With children and friends
Emails and papers
Urging us to remember
Our obligations
We created to get something
We thought we needed
Then
And now must be filed
Calendared
Remembered

Love requires none of this
Or at least not this love
To think of you is effortless
You are already there
To remember you is joy
To anticipate you is happiness

To be ready for you
Is pleasure without duty
I simply am
With full heart
Not alone
But full of you
Everywhere

Dearest Fleur

Dearest Fleur,

My very dearest asked me to write you a note. I was both excited and hesitant. What could I possibly say to the pleasure core of my love? How do I address you? What level to speak since before, my communications have all been by touch. Yes, the brain is the home of all physical pleasure, but you are so special, working in exquisite harmony with the brain. I tremble at the memories – so many – of our play together. We make beautiful, beautiful pictures. Stories and music unfold. We take journeys together. We create worlds together. We touch the formerly untouchable. We resist; then surrender to the waves of sensation. We ride the sensations mindless of all but the abundance of love.

I do not know what it is like for you and yet, there are times, when such togetherness could not possibly exist without such knowledge and I have been inducted into your soul, your breath, your skin, your sensation. I feel your wetness all the way through my hand, racing up my arm and then down to my pulsing pleasure where I can only mutely cry out in joy and shed my tears into you, on you. I touch you and the world is everything, the kingdoms have united, our possibilities are endless, our joy boundless, our love unassailable, our desires unquenchable… warmth spreading and spreading, hearts beating, breaths catching until a moment gives way to a second of rest and we start again. The tickling, teasing, lazy finger caressing the center of erotic softness that gathers tension like a storm about to erupt into lightening which hangs in suspense supported by rolling thunder, again and again. I feel your yearning, your sheer yielding, your overwhelming goodness and I am a man who has been given an angel – rescued from the banal, stripped of pretension, stripped of masks. I am left with only the self who has wanted you since all time. The self that must reveal itself without hesitation, without deprecation, without artificial trapping – in honesty as much as possible.

And what honesty is this – this drive to consume you and be consumed? But not the glutton's consumption but the consumption of life itself, the energy and power of the universe, in hand, in mouth, around me, in you. I will take it all. I will give it all. We want it all.

Thank you for reading this.

Your true love

The Poetry

The poetry
Of old men
Filled with gentle
regret
Yet
Simple
Appreciation
For small miracles
The seashells
On the beach
Free for taking
Perhaps not studied
But alive
For a brief
Light
Of perfect attention
Before the aches
And pains
Of living well
Or not so well
At all
Startled up
Like gulls
Settle
And land

We All Want Magic In Our Lives

We all want magic in our lives.
Thank god I found you
Heard you
Listened to you
Saw you
The veil was lifted
The search was ended
And I am left with me
With the right you
Today
This moment
And if this is magic
Then magic exists
Like grace
Descending
Like the sun
Burning off the haze
All beyond my power
But to receive

I never wanted a life of ease
I wanted a life of love
And creation
Of bringing something from nothing
Of feeling the universe
Flow through my fingers and body
And my mind singing songs
Given by ancestors
Not from will power and intent
I want the sweat of having climbed
A mountain
That leaves me breathless

From its beauty and view
And if I'm lucky
Touching you
With intense love
And hearing your breath
Acknowledge all of me
As I am

My True Heart Is Now In Charge

My true heart is now in charge
It opens my understanding
To you my lover
In unknowable ways
My true heart expanding
Scars replaced with simple wisdom
The warmth of love protecting
Our simple joy together
The triumph over fear
The disappointments of the past
The disappointments of self
The disappointments of others
The cocktail of emotions stirred by pain
Mysteriously healing
It is likely
that when I am not looking
My ego brain
May cry out
In panic again
Pushing the old
Buttons of defense
It was in charge
Once for too long
My true heart
Knows better
And slowly
Sings the calming songs

My Heart

My heart
Feels the peace
As I remember you
Followed
By relief
That you
Are still here
Still my love
Still my lover
Still my friend
Still I cry
And the peace
Returns
Smiling

If I Take The Time

If I take the time
When you are gone
To feel you
Here and now
Your perfume
Your touch
Your fullness
Your curves
The light in your eyes
In your being
In your soul
I fall in love
All over again

Day Is Flying By

Day is flying by
Head down
Focused and intent
Letting myself
Go ahead
Get excited
At the sheer joy
Of playing
And learning

I go for coffee
And suddenly
I feel the warmth
Of you
In the kitchen
My heart
Remembers to smile
Life is not rushing
As I hold your
Wonderful love
Like a small
Precious breathing
Living thing
Close as I can
To protect it
From the harm's way

Yes, time is speeding
Too fast for my life
Too fast for us
But not fast enough
Till l see you
Again

Alone Today

Alone today
Which is good
A man should be
Alone
Sometimes
To stop the noise
That is shouting
In his ear
Demanding
Emotional payoffs
For a life
In process
Unknown

No magic
In my coffee
To lift the fog
No lover's touch
To quell the fears
Of the dark
A sense of movement
Beginning
To grip me

Her scent
Thankfully lingers
Her voice
Alive and clear
They guide me
To the shores
Of real things
Beautiful
And kind

Not A Day Goes By

Not a day goes by
Without a moment
Of grace
Where I realize
Just how blessed
I am
To have you
In my life
Today

I offer my
Song
Of thanks
To the gods
Who made you
Who put us
Together
On this path
To walk
Shoulder to shoulder
Hand in hand
And if they listen
And if they feel
The common man's
Heart
May the heavens
Feel the small
Spreading ripple
Of joy
From mine

Cat Hiding In A Cupboard

Cat hiding in a cupboard
God knows what she is thinking
But dark and away
Is what she needs
She takes care of her self
The best she can

And she reminds me
To take care of you
To take care of me
The best I can
The heart is speaking
And knows
What is important

The lump in my throat
When I found her
And could not wait to call you
The desire to share my relief
The desire to hold you
What is important
Not so hard

You are my love

Sitting Here Guitar In Hand

Sitting here guitar in hand
And you dance across my mind
A flirt and a knowing smile
Your warm hand
Brushes my cheek
And then you are off
And I am left
Wanting
You

What Is Love Now

What is love now

 The breath I catch
When I see you
The warmth I feel
Behind me at night
The tender kiss
Of greeting
Of goodbye
The full embrace
The letting go
The letting in
The shared life
Cooking side by side
Eating side by side
Reviewing the day
Reading aloud
Bringing humor
Being there when I am not
Caring for wounds
That can and cannot
Be seen

Creating together
A life of joy
Of kindness
And pleasure
Every day richer
Because you are there
Blessed angel
Because you are there
My heart sings
All day

You Are Sleeping

You are sleeping
When I realize
I so easily take our love
For granted
Which is good
It is always there
Gently filling me with
Light and comfort
But bad
Because I must not
Forget my desire
To please you
To surprise you
To show myself
To be available
Heart and soul
Every day

Maybe This Rush

Maybe this rush
Through life
Is just what is needed
Now
Embracing life
With both arms
Reminds me
Of you

I could see us
Gardens and flowers
Dogs and cats
Goats being stubborn
With time for poetry
And music
And cooking
And loving

Maybe this rush
Is preparing us
To handle even more
Tender touches
On your silken cheek
Dancing in the dark
The ficus tree leaves
Stretched across the sky
Gently moving our rhythm
The air caressing
Our breaths undisturbed

Even full with love
Their remain questions
To be answered
Journeys to be taken

Tastes awaiting discovery
Jasmine aromas
Scented foreign streets
Tripped upon a thousand years
Warm air kissing skin
Awake

Maybe

I Miss You

I miss you
Your German humor
Your clever language
Your sincere desire
To please them.
They are in heaven
As am I
With the thought
Of you.

May our love
Guide us
And show us
Our best selves
Making our lives
The joyful dance
They were meant
To be

May our love
Warm us
Like the sun
On a cool and clear
Winter day
Letting us breathe
Just a little easier
For that moment
Of life's tender
Embrace

Alone Tonight

Alone tonight
My ears still pulsing
From music
My face lined
From the years
Of smiling
And hiding behind
Raised eyebrows
Feigning interest

You are in the next room
Sleeping peacefully
While I sit
Trying to catch
My breath

Today we read
Out loud
A friend's candid writing
A gift of love
About her love
Her passion
For a husband
Long gone

I carried her joy
And her heartache
For the rest of the day
And felt again
Our first days' joy
And happiness
And loving discovery

I swore I would sing
My love songs
To you
Every day
And I am desolate
I have not
I thought I must
Do better
Than just describe
The simple truths
In me
Between us
The rapture I feel
Kissing you
Touching you
The simple pleasure
Of your gaze upon me
Frank and honest
Taking me in
Holding me
Like the most natural
Thing in the world
But which I turn away
Afraid to really see
Because what if it's
Not really there?
And when I really see
I see more love
More love
Than I thought
I could bear
And your beautiful heart
Which should know better
But refuses to give up
Not yet
Not today

I have only my heart
And soul
To give you
And you received them
On our first day
With beautiful gentleness
And kindness
And fiery passion
And I will give them
Again and again
To you my angel
My love
My friend
My muse
And by the grace
Of the gods
My wife

I love you
More than words
More than touches
More than the stars

An Old Business Aquaintance

An old business acquaintance
Hopes if I am well
I tell him
I am having
The time of my life
And with one phrase
Sum up my new life
With you
With music
This is the time
When living has new meaning
When loving demands
All my soul and heart
When a life so lived
Is so big
The past and the future
Are distant faint echoes
Now, only now
In your arms
Your kiss the beginning
And the end
Of my travels
Your warm touch
The awakening
Your spirit
Guides me
To life
This time

Missing You

Missing you
First pain
Then pleasure
I will see you
Again
Soon
Tonight
Like Christmas
Every day
Your presence
Wrapped
Beauty beneath
Style
Quiet certainty
Really
Too much
And never enough
For this
Simple man

My Cat Says

My cat says
Look at the tree
As the sun sets
I do
It is life itself
Dark leaves trembling
At the bottom
Light shooting across
The top
Green leaves shimmering
Blue sky
Clear as noon
I am lifted
My spirit rising
Love in my heart
I await thee

How Many Ways

How many ways
Can a man
Tell his love
That he loves her

Try an action
Sometimes
Loving words
Come easy for this man
But actions take
Something more
That I sometimes
Forget I have

So I'm off to buy dinner
That you might like
And find some time
To listen
And hold
Your hopes
And new dreams

Home Late

Home late
You are asleep
As it should be
I catch my breath
Life is good
All my rushing
Makes me lose sight
Of how beautiful
You are
How incredible
You are
You with me
Life is magic
Don't forget
Don't forget
Don't forget
As if a simple chant
Could teach me
How much I have
How much I want
How much you are

Lovers Approach

Lovers approach
A child bouquet
Firework colors
Softly fading
To reverse

Lovers' hands touching
Full of liquid warmth
A good whiskey
Smiling
Erasing distance

Lovers embrace
The howl of
Massive power
A run to the edge
Of the soul's galaxy
To see a universe

Lovers life
A quiet stream
Music of nature
Along a gentle path
Cushioned by pine needles
Trees filter light
Wet leaf perfume
Carrying hearts
Scarred but growing
Lighter

Lovers climb
The trail is higher
The buffers down
Rocks to be avoided
The unrelenting brightness
Warming
Exposing
Lifting spirits
To true light

Some Days

Some days
I can't believe
I share my life
With you
This unbelievable you
Warm spirit
Gentle grace
Beautiful kindness
Loving touches
On every level
That made me drunk
With you
The very first day

I resolve to treasure
Every morning
Every day
Every evening
Until the last day
Finally passes
So there will be
No tears of regret
To make bitter
The unthinkable loss
Of what was never mine
But so freely given

One's Ability To Love

One's ability to love
In fullness
With electricity
With enraptured heart
The smell of the loved one
Intoxicating
The sense of being home
Of finally holding
And being held
Safety and mystery
Fear and comfort
Should not be forsaken

So many will enter
The temple and lose
Their way
And for some
No temple will appear
Or they will lie
In hiding
But I have found you
And have learned
To dance
And pray
For the magic
Of eternity

My Lips

My lips
Graze your hair
A fleeting moment
Your natural heat
Rising to meet me
This is enough
This should be
Enough
As you walk
To your car
To remind me
That all my choices
Brought me here
Even the bad ones
The ones that hurt
The ones that brought
Grace and quiet
The ones that whispered
Life could be different
The ones that reflected
A soul in waiting
I no longer wait for you
Like I did
When I didn't know you
Waiting is still a part
Of my life
Our life

But it's different now
I can still feel
Your warm hand
In mine

Just A Sheet Of Paper

Just a sheet of paper
To start the day
No small matters
Happy to be working
Fingers dancing
Well, fingers punching
Whack-a-mole
With scattered thoughts
To be precise
I write in fragments
That are not prose
My thoughts run on
But I can hear them
This way

One's ability to love
In fullness
With electricity
With enraptured heart
The smell of the loved one
Intoxicating
The sense of being home
Of finally holding
And being held
Safety and mystery
Fear and comfort
Should not be forsaken

So many will enter
The temple and lose
Their way
And for some
No temple will appear
Or they will lie

In hiding
But I have found you
And have learned
To dance
And pray
For the magic
Of eternity

Small Smooth Thoughts

Small smooth thoughts
Of you
Tumbled over and over
Mine and mine again
Shine like smiles
A caress that kisses
The warm hand
The quiet mind
Breaths free
Easy heart crying
Soft tears
Softer skin
Upon my cheek
Your heat
My favorite comfort
Your lover's eye
Gently telling me
That you are truly
There
With me

Thought I Might Be

Thought I might be
Someone who knew
All about relationships
Since I've studied them
Trying to master them
Spending enormous time
With lost causes

Then you find me
And I feel
The impact of
Destiny's collision
Planets kicked out of orbit
Stars hurled further
As the universe expands
Blindingly fast
With terrible power

Left trembling
Thoughts gone
Alive with you

There Isn't Much Time

There isn't much time
This time
But some time
Better than no time
To love you
A life time

The do-over
Is never possible
But for now
I believe
In miracles
And light
This time

You Ask Me

You ask me
What does love mean
And I struggle
To answer
After all my words
Years of turning phrases
Decades of practiced nuance
A simple definition
Eludes me
A simple word
Defies me
Of course
For one must read
All the words of
All the secret books
To understand
Their title: Love

But to begin
Love is a magic formula
Between two persons
That allows their entirety
To rest in the arms of the other
In transcendence
To experience the perfection
Of union - spirit, mind and body
Love is desire beyond the flesh
Love is the soul's song to another
Love is the understanding
That maybe you don't understand
Anything the way
You thought you did
Love is calmness and beauty
Wrapped in warmth

Love is giving
Love is receiving
Love is not knowing
Whether you are giving or receiving
Love is looking at the mirror of self
Created by your lover
And seeing all that is possible
With gentle forgiveness
Love is creating stories
For both and believing them
Until they are true
Love is facing the world
Side by side
Hand in hand
Eyes on the horizon
Love is sharing
The daily moments
That were always there
But now made priceless
By being together
Love is waking up
To the glow of another
Love is kindness
Even when darkness visits
Love is joy
You didn't know before
Love is pain
You didn't know before
Love is happiness
For no reason except
That your lover
Is in your life
Love is discovering
You are each an ocean
Deeper than imagined
Largely unexplored
With favorite places

And secrets
That might never yield
Love is a shooting star
Suspended in time
Across the dark skies
Our breath caught
Again and again
Love is realizing
How frail life is
How frail our thinking
How frail our coupling
Of intent and action
Love is a story written
Every day
Love is a story never finished
Love is a glance across a room
That holds everything
That says everything
Love is a smile
Only for you
Love is a look
Only for you
Love mocks are fears
Pushes our precious boundaries
Toys with our conceptions
Laughs at our imperfections
Love is so large
It grows our hearts to hold it
Love is so small
It lives in every cell of our being
Love is so fast
It comes to us before we know it
Love is so slow
We can spend a lifetime
Waiting for its kiss
Love is what we make
Love is what makes us

Love is none of this
Love is all of this
Love is you
Love is us

Thinking About Dreams

Thinking about dreams:

Dreams only fail if we stop working for them.
There are many reasons to stop.
There will always be many reasons to stop.
It may be a correct response to stop if we realize that the dream is not what we thought it was, that it was not the dream we wanted after all or that we have a new dream.
Dreams are changing constantly.
When dreams are accomplished, a new one will take its place.
We only hear, see or feel our dreams when we are quiet and receptive.
Being quiet and receptive can happen when we are standing in the middle of stress, challenge, noise and chaos.
When the dream is ready, it will push to be heard.
Ignoring the little quiet voices that ask us to do a certain something (which often appears like a whim or something different than usual) will kill the voices telling you about the really good important dreams.
Sitting doing nothing is good for dreaming.
Doing something new is good for dreaming.
Letting go of the "shoulds" and "oughts" is good for dreaming.

Being loved whole-heartedly and loving whole-heartedly is good for dreaming.
If we think about what others will think when we take steps towards our dreams, we will be carrying a lifetime of critical thought to our tender dream and likely killing it.
The dream may only be there to teach you about the next dream.
Your heart knows the meaning of your dream; you do not.
Our dreams are ours alone.
Dreams about money are disguised dreams – the real dream is what we would do with the money.
Be aware of the moments that make you feel like anything is possible. They are little states of grace that bless our dreams.
Be aware of the activities that make you feel like you are living the dream… you are.
Not living your dream is like not being yourself.
If you don't believe in your dream, you don't believe in the wisdom of you.
Because you are not clothed in every aspect of the dream (e.g., you have not won an Oscar for acting or a Grammy for songwriting yet) does not mean you are not living your dream.
When we are tired is not the time to ask about the reality of our dream.
When we compare ourselves to others with what appears to be a similar dream, our egos will lose help and try and quit.
You and your dream are unique.

Dream comparison is death, or at least really unhelpful.
The dream of living life with style, grace and wisdom does not depend on any events, things or people other than oneself.
Dreaming is not thinking…

To Wake Up To You

To wake up to you
Next to me
Warm and soft
The familiar hum
Of the day
Complex layers
Harmonies and dissonance
Espresso machine
Armed and ready
Cat asking
If I'm up and steady
Easing into the day
Gratitude for you
Fills my soul
With music
Gentle happy
Meadow music
Fresh with pine
Notes of melting snow
Clouds of warm soil
Flocks of tender flowers
Water splashing to the sea
You and me
You and me

www.ingramcontent.com/pod-product-compliance
Lightning Source LLC
Chambersburg PA
CBHW031358160426
42813CB00090B/3217/J